D0048547

FROM RENTING
TO BUYING

A Basic Guide to First Time
Home Buying and Ownership

BEN STEFAN

ISBN: 978-1-54390-729-2 (print)
ISBN: 978-1-54390-730-8 (ebook)

TABLE OF CONTENTS

1. INTRODUCTION

B uying your first home marks an exciting time. Reaching this milestone in your life is an outstanding accomplishment. It doesn't matter whether the home is a 10,000-square-foot estate or an 800-square-foot bungalow, owning your own single-family home is a great achievement.

Buying a home, however, can be a challenging process for many, especially first-time homebuyers. Among the many factors to consider are the search, negotiation, financing and closing processes as well as all the things you need to know once you actually own the house. Although this can be a lot to digest, this book will guide you as a first-time homebuyer and provide as a reference source to help you through the process of buying and owning your first home.

Once you close on your home, you should be proud of yourself for taking the big step toward doing what it takes to become a homeowner. This marks the beginning of a new era for you and your family. Embrace the possibilities and envision all the things you will do and can do once you move in. This book is your guide along the way.

2. FINDING YOUR HOME

Because you are reading this, you probably have made the decision to buy a home. This is an exciting decision. Congratulations! The next step is to search for the home you will love. If you have decided to buy a home, you probably have a general idea of where you want to live. Typically, most homebuyers look to buy a home within a 50-mile radius of their primary source of employment. Next comes the fun part of weighing all of your options and narrowing them all down to the one neighborhood in which you want live. The next sections provide a breakdown of considerations at the state, municipal, and neighborhood level.

State level

If you live in an area with multiple state borders or in a tri-state region, consider the state in which you would like to reside. Consider the following:

- State fiscal condition and taxes: Is the state under heavy financial stress or debt? Could you face large tax increases in the near term? It is a good idea to educate yourself about what may be coming down the road fiscally in the state you are considering.

- State economy: Does the state promote small business? Does it encourage commerce? Is the population benefiting from a vibrant economy?

- Transportation accessibility and infrastructure: Does the state have a well laid-out infrastructure for transportation, highways, railways, and airports? Can you conveniently get to where you want to go? Is the infrastructure updated and functional? Can you see yourself easily getting from place to place?

Municipal level

After you have determined the state in which you will buy your home, you now need to focus on the town or city. Consider the following:

- Town amenities: What does the town have to offer? Is there a park, beach, or municipal golf course? Is there a train station? Can you access the highway? Are there commuter lots? What about restaurants? How's the nightlife? Does the town provide things that will make your life easier and enjoyable? For most people, these amenities are critical.

- Town fiscal condition: Research how the municipality is doing fiscally. Is the town burdened with debt? If so, this debt could cause the amenities to suffer and the tax rate or mill levy to increase. Examine the town taxes, property tax, and school taxes so that you understand the costs of the town you are considering.

- Town crime: Is the town safe? Do they have a good police force and fire department?

- Town school system: How is the school system? Even if you do not have kids, a good town school system is desirable for many people and helps keep property values stable or improving.

Neighborhood level

Now that you have narrowed down the municipalities you like, your focus should turn to the neighborhood. Consider the following:

- Community: Are you looking for a tight-knit neighborhood where everyone knows one another? Or do you like more independence? How close are the homes to each other? How big or small are the parcels? Do you want to be on a cul-de-sac, private street, main road, or busy road?

- Commercial area: Can you be in proximity to a commercial corridor? Can you live in a commercial area, say, in a condo or townhouse in the downtown area? Can you tolerate noise, activity and traffic?

- Road: Can you live on a highly trafficked road? Does it have sidewalks? Is it a high-speed road, does it have a lot of traffic congestion?

- Gated community: Some towns have gated communities and crime watches that are great options to consider, if available.

- Golf course community: Are you a golfer? Would you like to live on a golf course and have golfing amenities within the community? It may be worth researching towns that feature these communities and neighborhoods.

To gather information on all these factors, you can conduct research online, check local online news archives for articles, visit state and municipal websites, research reports on crime, and most important, drive around the desired target areas. Get a feel for the people, flow, cleanliness, demographic, and population, and see whether you can envision yourself living there. Ask your mind, heart, and gut whether this is a place where you would be comfortable investing and living. Your gut feeling will tell you whether it is the right spot for you, and when you have recognized that feeling, it will help you commit to a decision on your location.

The home

Last, the obvious part is finding the right house. Many people begin their home searches online with websites like Zillow, Trulia, Realtor.com, and local realtor websites. This is a good way to start. When you are narrowing in on a few properties you like, your next step will be to hire a realtor. It is important to find a realtor in whom you have great comfort.

Ask around to locate someone who will represent you well. If you have friends in the area who recently went through the buying process, ask them who they used and whether they would refer their realtor. If you know real estate experts in the area who are involved in construction, home design, commercial brokerage, or architecture, ask who they would refer. Real estate markets are deeply interconnected. Many real estate professionals within the market have worked with each other and know good realtors who may be a great fit for you. You also can find a brokerage you like based on their marketing, performance, and presence in the market. If you don't have a referral, you can call the brokerage you like, and they can place you with an agent who would be a good fit.

When you start talking to the agents, interview them and make sure you are getting an agent who understands your needs. When an agent is helping you find a home, they are on your team, not on your payroll. This means that you do not have to pay your representing agent. The agent is paid by the selling homeowner through a percentage commission of the sale price. So, for example, if you purchase a home for $100,000, the owner would need to pay a 5% commission (2.5% to the listing agent, 2.5% to the buyer's agent), totaling $5,000 at the closing. That is how your representing agent gets paid.

When you sign an agreement with an agent, it generally is an exclusive right for that agent to represent you. This means that once the agreement is signed, it protects the agent from you deciding to run off and find another representing agent. If you do that, and you find a home and close on it, the original agent still is entitled to the commission. This will cause problems and delay the closing, so ensure that you are comfortable with your representing agent before you sign an exclusive rights form.

When looking for the right house, you have many things to consider. You look for the best location, style, square footage, number of beds and baths, number of garage bays, yard size, and other factors that are important to you. Only you are going to know what you are going to like. All of these things you are considering are going to affect an important factor: price. You need to know what you can afford and what your price range will be to get the search process under way.

Understand your price range

If you don't know what you can afford, answer the following questions to help you determine how much you can spend on a new home:

- How much do you currently pay in rent each month? Is it a strain for you to make that payment? Or can you afford to make higher payments? Use this amount as your baseline for monthly payment consideration.

- How much liquidity (cash) do you currently have available? You need to consider liquidity because when you are looking to buy a home, you most likely will be seeking financing (mortgage) to help you purchase the house. If you do this, you will need to put a down payment on the house. Depending on whether you are eligible for a first-time homebuyers program, this down payment can range from as little as 3% to more than 25% of the purchase price. To learn more about first-time homebuyer financing opportunities, discuss options with your lender or bank. This process is explained in more detail in Chapter 4, "Understanding the Financing and Process of Getting a Mortgage."

- What is your mortgage payment? The easiest way to do this is to go online and conduct a search on Google for "Mortgage Payment Calculator." You will get websites that will calculate this for you. These calculators will factor in going percentage rates, give you a term option, and ask how much you wish to borrow. You will need to input the amount of the purchase price of the home. Once you do that, press the "Calculate" button and the monthly payment amount will be displayed. If you can afford it, can't afford it, or can afford more, decrease or increase the desired loan amount and recalculate. Play around with the numbers until you identify a general ballpark of what you can afford. It is important to understand that this will calculate only the payment on the mortgage based on the terms you input. When you buy a home, you may have other costs that are in addition to your mortgage payment like taxes and insurance. Depending on which site you go to, they may factor in taxes and insurance.

By answering these questions, you will get a basic idea of what your price range is for a new home. This will help you so you aren't blindsided by price and don't waste time searching for a home you cannot afford.

Once you have an idea of your price range, you can start to narrow down on some homes. When you begin looking at homes you like, you will need to observe a few important things about the building structure and condition. Whether the home is newer, older, or historical, you always should observe the structure and condition of the home.

Building structure and condition

Foundation

Typically, you cannot judge the integrity of the home's foundation by photos online. When you do your first walk-through, be sure to go to the basement to inspect the foundation walls and sill plates (sills). Look for the obvious signs like crumbling concrete, crumbling cinder blocks, and water and drainage issues compromising the foundation walls. Also observe the condition of the sills. Sills are the pieces of wood that sit directly on top of the foundation walls on which the structure of the home rests. Make sure these are not rotted and that you don't see any termite issues. An indication of termite infestation in the basement would be mud and vein-like trails on and around the wood, as well as dried-out rotted wood. If you do not see any visible signs, you can tap the wood sills with a hammer to test the strength of the wood to determine whether rot or termites have caused damage. If you identify termite issues, but you really like the home, calling an exterminator and carpenter should be one of your highest priorities so they can inspect prior to closing. If you still are

considering buying the house, have them give you an assess-
ment to exterminate and to make any necessary repairs before
you purchase the home, this can be a point of negotiation
when agreeing on a purchase price.

Foundation Structure

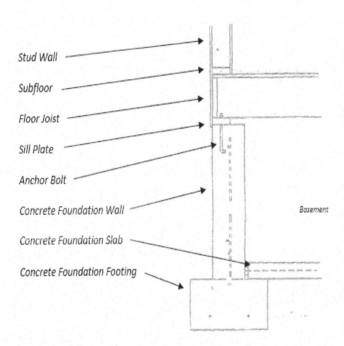

Fig. 1. Foundation framing, sills and concrete

If the home does not have a basement and is built on
footings, you may be able to access a crawlspace underneath
the home. If you can find a way to get under the house, check

the footings and sills. Crawling in a small dirty crawlspace is not optimal, so do the best you can and dress appropriately. Opt for jeans and a long sleeve shirt over a frilly dress and bring a flashlight. This will help you navigate comfortably and safely in the dark areas to do a quick scan of the space.

Structure

Even when you are looking online at photos, you can sense whether work is needed and whether the home has any structural red flags. This doesn't exclude new homes. Newer homes can be built poorly, resulting in a compromise in the integrity of the building structure. Usually, when a new home is built, municipal inspections are required during the construction process so that the structure is being built to code and is safe. However, this may not always be the case. This is especially true if it looks like a newer renovation was made to an older home. It is always a good idea to check whether any permits have been "pulled" for construction, licensed contractors performed the work, and everything was done in compliance with building codes. You can do this by checking with the town or city's building department that manages the permit and inspection process.

If you are buying a home that was built recently, try to find out who the builder was, review their website, and see how they build their homes along with searching for reviews.

If the builder doesn't have a website, this is not an issue, just ask the builder for references to call and talk to those home-owners. In some cases, these homeowners may have you over to their house for a walk-through. If you are looking at brand new homes, make sure the builder provides a guarantee for at least 6 months after closing and that the home has a certificate of occupancy (CO) issued by the town. A CO is a certification that all inspections were passed during the construction pro-cess and that the home is certifiably habitable.

When looking at older or historic homes, always exam-ine the basement joists and support columns or beams. These include the floor joists, beams, steel, 2 x 8s, or 2 x 10s, or the Trus Joint I's (TJIs) that can be found in newer homes. This framing holds up the floor and interior structure of the home. Check the condition of the sills as well. Do your best to identify any serious cracks, warping, and rot that might indicate a potential hazard when examining the structure.

House Framing/Structure

Fig. 2. House framing / structural diagrams

If you are interested in a particular home, you should hire a professional home inspector who will give you a thorough report on the home. This includes crawling into that dirty crawl space to test the footings, sills, structure, electric, plumbing, ventilation, septic system, and any other items to report on the habitability of the home. Depending on the size of the home and area in which you are located, inspectors will charge approximately $300 or more for an inspection and full report.

Always be aware of rot, deterioration, termites, and areas that seem to be over-settled. These are obvious structural red flags, but they do get overlooked. If you can observe these things, it will help you know when to move on to the next house, avoid wasting time, and save you money so that you don't unnecessarily hire an inspector.

If you fall in love with a home that has a lot of structural issues, you can move forward with the purchase, but you should bring in contractors to give you estimates on what it will cost to fix the problems so you can determine whether the house still meets your financial parameters. If you decide to move forward, factor such costs into the offer you make. This can save you a considerable amount of money.

3. WHAT YOU NEED TO KNOW ONCE YOU FIND THE HOME YOU LIKE

Once you reach the point at which you think you have found your home, you need to understand your costs going forward. Would you like to make any improvements to the home immediately before you take occupancy? Or right when you move? If so, you should make a budget, so that you understand all of the numbers going into this investment. Also, it is important to understand your operating costs for the home. What are the annual property taxes? Know the insurance costs as well as the electric (summer and winter), heating, water, cable, and property maintenance costs. Also, investigate any potential upcoming expenses for the home. For example, when you have the contractors come over, get an estimate on how long the roof will last. Is it a 20-year-old roof that needs to be replaced in 3 years? Or is it relatively new?

How old is the septic system and how is it working? If the home has a septic system, spend time investigating it because if you need a new septic system, it can be a significant expense. Make sure your inspector checks the system and have a septic pump company check it for you as well.

If you are looking to make some upfront improvements to the home, you can get quotes from local contractors on the projects you are considering and you can build a budget for total work before you close on your home. This depends on the time you have and the level of urgency behind the purchase. If the home is in high demand, and it is urgent to make an offer, you may not have this luxury. But, if you can dig into the numbers, you can be more decisive and make a more informed offer, which can help protect you from unexpected costs and aggravation.

Remember, when you find that special home you really like, and you are at the point at which you want to make an offer, bring in an inspector to professionally examine the property. Although you have done your homework and now understand and know what to look for, you are not a professional. Search online for local inspectors and read reviews about their work. Make sure you get a qualified professional to examine your home. They may find something you overlooked, and if you catch things early, you can avoid big issues later. The cost to hire a qualified inspector will be well worth the peace of mind.

4. UNDERSTAND THE FINANCING AND THE PROCESS OF GETTING A MORTGAGE

During the home search process, if you need to obtain a mortgage, begin digging into sources of financing. If possible, try to find a bank or mortgage company that will pre-approve you for a mortgage. If you can get preapproval, it can help expedite the closing process when you do find a home. You may be wondering how you can get preapproved if you haven't found a home yet. The banks will preapprove you if you provide them with general information on the house you are searching for, mortgage amount requested, and your personal financial information. If you have narrowed your ideal home down to be a three-bedroom, two-bathroom home in a certain town at a price range of $350,000 to $400,000, the bank can work with that information and your personal information to preapprove your request for financing.

With that said, ensure that you have your personal information organized. The bank typically will ask for three years of personal tax returns, three years of any business tax returns if applicable, three years of any audited financial statements, a net worth statement, and brokerage and bank statements, as well as proof of income. The bank uses all of this information to perform the proper analysis to assess the risk of lending to you. Send all of this information to your lender of choice before you find your home. If you have all of your financial ducks in a row and have financing preapproval before you lock in on a house, it will help you be more efficient and less stressed throughout the closing process.

Understanding the bank's review process

The following glossary will provide you with an understanding of a few terms bankers like to throw around to sound smart. Securing your loan should not be an exercise in intimidation, so let's get you grounded in the basics. The following important definitions will help you understand the bank's review process:

Underwriting: Analysis conducted by the bank to determine whether the loan can be granted. This usually considers your income, the asset or home you want to buy, and your credit score.

Due Diligence: During the underwriting process, the bank needs to ensure that they have all the necessary documentation to seek approval and close the loan. They refer to this as "due diligence."

LTV: This is the loan-to-value ratio. The LTV is calculated by dividing the requested loan amount by the appraised value of the home.

Principal: This is the actual money borrowed from the bank. So when they say, "You have an outstanding principal balance of $200,000," this means you have $200,000 remaining to repay to the bank. This is separate from any interest balances.

Interest: This is the cost of borrowing money from the bank. They will charge you interest when you borrow from them so they can make money.

Rate: This determines the amount of money you will be paying to the bank in interest payments. It is calculated off your outstanding principal balance.

Capital: Money you have available.

Mortgage or Loan: These are interchangeable terms for the debt that is needed to buy a home.

Escrow: To place funds or documents in custody or a trust.

Lenders will rely heavily on their financial analysis when seeking approval for your loan. Below are some assessments the bank will focus on:

Debt-to-Income Ratio

In regard to your financial condition, the banks will rely heavily on your debt-to-income (DTI) ratio. This ratio is the comparison of your mortgage on the home and your monthly debt obligations divided by how much income you are generating each month. For example, if the mortgage you are requesting requires a monthly payment of $1,528 plus $500 in taxes and $141 in insurance (taxes and insurance typically are included, but it could depend on the lender), your total home mortgage payment would be $2,169. Then the bank will total all your additional monthly debt obligations, including credit cards, car loans, and other debt responsibilities. They then will add this amount to your mortgage payment obligation and calculate your DTI ratio. The example is illustrated in Table 1:

Debt to Income Ratio Example		
Mortgage	$	1,528
Taxes	$	500
Insurance	$	141
Credit Cards	$	1,000
Student Loans	$	200
Car Loans	$	200
Other Debt	$	50
Total Debt	$	3,619
Monthly Income	$	10,000
DTI		0.36

Table 1. DTI Ratio Chart

Based on the example in Table 1, the DTI is 0.36. The lower the DTI number, the more appealing you will be to a bank for approval. Generally, banks want to see a DTI ratio below 0.40. They can be flexible, however, depending on other factors.

Credit worthiness

Banks also will look at your credit score during the under-writing process to determine approval. When the bank runs a credit report on you, the report will show three scores: your

Equifax, Experian, and TransUnion scores. These scores can range from 300 to 850, with 850 being the best. The higher the scores, the more appealing you will be to a lender.

Credit reports contain information about your payment history, loans, debt, credit cards, and other financial payment records. They also provide information on whether you have been arrested, sued, or involved in bankruptcy. The information in these reports helps lenders determine whether they want to lend to you and the terms under which they can lend.

It is important to periodically check on your credit report to ensure that your information is reported accurately, that no inconsistencies appear on your credit report, or that no fraudulent accounts have been opened in your name. You are entitled to a free credit report from each agency (Equifax, Experian, and TransUnion) once every year.

Collateral

Banks lend borrowers money for all types of things—to buy houses, buildings, and airplanes, or to start a new business or even purchase art, the list goes on depending on the kind of lender. When the bank lends money, they not only assess the borrower's financial condition and credit worthiness but also assess the borrower's "collateral." The collateral is the asset being purchased—in this case, it is the home. This collateral is a safeguard that helps ensure that the lender will get its money back if the borrower fails to pay. When the loan closes, the bank becomes the lienholder on the property while you own your home. If, however you default, the bank has rights to start legal action to begin the foreclosure process. For this reason, the bank will underwrite loans with an emphasis on the LTV ratio. The further the loan amount is below the value of the home, the more comfortable the bank will be with the asset and their security.

How mortgage payments work

You might be wondering how mortgage payments work. And if you need to borrow a certain amount, you also need to know how much your monthly mortgage payments will be. The following example will help you understand how a mortgage works:

Let's say you found a home and you are going to purchase it for $400,000. Depending on your terms, the bank will finance a certain percentage of this purchase price. They first will get an appraisal on the home and determine its "market value." For the sake of this example, let's say it is valued at $400,000. Under the terms of this loan, the bank will finance 80% of the value (the LTV), which is $320,000. This means that you need to make an $80,000 down payment. This deposit is considered your equity in the home.

Table 2 provides a hypothetical example of the terms that you and your bank have agreed upon:

Equity	$	80,000
Mortgage	$	320,000
Total Home Value	$	400,000
Interest Rate		4.00%
Term		30
Amortization		30
Monthly Payment	$	1,528
Annual Payment	$	18,505

Table 2. Hypothetical mortgage terms.

- The interest rate is determined by an index used by the bank, like a LIBOR (London Inter Bank Offered Rate) or FHLBB (Federal Home Loan Bank of Boston) index plus the spread for the bank. The spread is the difference between the index rate and the actual interest rate you are charged. This is how banks make money lending to you. The index plus the spread is the cost of capital.

- The term is the amount of time until the loan "matures," that is to say, when the balance becomes due in full. Let's say that you originated the mortgage in 2016 and you had a 30-year term, your "maturity date," the date at which your loan becomes due, would be in the year 2046. It is expected that the loan should be paid on or before maturity.

- The amortization is how you pay down the principal and the interest. Each monthly payment you make goes to pay down the principal balance on your loan and the interest owed for having the loan. The payment is made up of a portion of principal and a portion of interest.

As you continue to pay your mortgage payments, your loan balance shrinks. Therefore, your interest payments on a smaller loan balance will get smaller over time. Because your monthly payment does not change, the portion of the payment that is applied to reducing your loan balance, or the "principal," becomes larger. This accelerates the rate at which you pay off the outstanding principal balance over time.

The amortization schedule is the set timeframe in which this pay down process occurs. So, if you had a 30-year amortization schedule, it would take 30 years to pay off the mortgage if you strictly followed the payment schedule.

This example has a principal loan balance of $320,000, a 4% interest rate, and a 30-year amortization schedule:

A	B	C	D	E
Outstanding Balance	Interest Payment	Principal Payment	Total Payment	Remaining Balance
$ 320,000	$ 1,067	$ 461	$ 1,528	$ 319,539
$ 319,539	$ 1,065	$ 463	$ 1,528	$ 319,076
$ 319,076	$ 1,064	$ 464	$ 1,528	$ 318,612
$ 318,612	$ 1,062	$ 466	$ 1,528	$ 318,146
$ 318,146	$ 1,060	$ 468	$ 1,528	$ 317,678

Fast forward 30 years to the last few months of the loan
(After 30 years / 360 monthly mortgage payments)

$ 4,368	$ 15	$ 1,513	$ 1,528	$ 2,855
$ 2,855	$ 10	$ 1,518	$ 1,528	$ 1,336
$ 1,336	$ 4	$ 1,524	$ 1,528	$ (187)

Fig. 3. Amortization schedule.

According to the example in Fig. 3,

A = The Outstanding Balance at the start of the loan.

B = The Interest Payment is the interest portion of your payment (the interest rate multiplied by the outstanding balance).

C = The Principal Payment is the difference in the Total Payment and Interest Payment.

D = The Total Payment is the fixed calculated payment based on the terms of the loan (it will be the same amount on every payment).

E = The Remaining Balance is what is left after each payment.

Observe how the principal payment is much larger toward the end and the interest is larger in the beginning. This is the math behind your amortizing mortgage.

When going through the mortgage process, bank fees and origination fees may be included. Depending on your lender, you may have room to negotiate these fees down. If you are in good standing with the bank, and have a great DTI, credit scores, and LTV, you will be an optimal customer for many banks. You can use this to your benefit to save on bank fees, so don't be bashful about requesting these savings. With these qualities, you can shop around for lenders and they will compete for your business.

Managing your mortgage payments

After you close on your home, you then will be responsible for paying your mortgage payments monthly. You likely will have arranged a payment structure with the bank that adds in your monthly loan payment monies, property tax, and insurance premiums. A lot of banks will do this to ensure that your tax payments do not become delinquent and their collateral (your home) is always insured in case of a catastrophic event. These tax and insurance payments will be collected with your mortgage payment and escrowed by the bank and then are paid by the bank to the relevant municipality and insurance company when payments are due. This way everything stays current. Consider the following example using the payment amount given in the previous example:

Assumptions for Payment on House

Estimated Annual Tax	$	6,000.00
Estimated Annual Insurance Premium	$	1,700.00
Monthly Mortgage Payment	$	1,528.00
Monthly Tax Payment	$	500.00
Monthly Insurance Payment	$	141.00
Total Monthly Payment	$	2,169.00

Fig. 4. Assumptions for house payments.

How to stay on top of your mortgage payments

Now that you know the amount of your total monthly payment, you will need to budget your funds appropriately. If possible, set up an automatic electronic payment system with your bank so that the funds can be withdrawn on each payment's due date. This will save you the hassle of writing a check every month. Life can get in the way of responsibilities, and if you forget about writing that check, then you are in a pickle. Remember, if you set up this automatic withdraw from your bank account, the bank will withdraw money from your account without a notification every month, so set a reminder for yourself on your phone a few days before the withdraw is scheduled so that you can make sure your account has sufficient funds before the amount is drawn. You want to avoid overdraft fees and a missed payment penalty.

Payment trick

If you want to pay off your mortgage as quickly as possible, without spending every penny you make, you can follow a simple trick that can accelerate your outstanding principal repayment. If you refer to the amortization schedule from earlier (Fig. 3), you'll remember that your monthly payment is split out into two portions: (1) your interest portion, and (2) your principal portion. If you create your own amortization schedule based on your loan terms or request one from your bank, you can track every payment of interest and principal you make. Now that you know that, here is the trick: *Apply the next month's principal portion in addition to your regular payment, for every payment, or whatever principal portion you can handle financially.* Look at this example:

Outstanding Balance	Interest Payment	Principal Payment	Total Payment	Remaining Balance
$ 320,000	$ 1,067	$ 461	$ 1,528	$ 319,539
$ 319,539	$ 1,065	$ 463	$ 1,528	$ 319,076
$ 319,076	$ 1,064	$ 464	$ 1,528	$ 318,612
$ 318,612	$ 1,062	$ 466	$ 1,528	$ 318,146
$ 318,146	$ 1,060	$ 468	$ 1,528	$ 317,678
$ 317,678	$ 1,059	$ 469	$ 1,528	$ 317,209
$ 317,209	$ 1,057	$ 471	$ 1,528	$ 316,738

Principal Paydown Acceleration		
Month 1 Payment	$	1,528
Next Months Principal Portion	$	463
Total Mortgage Payment for Month 1	$	1,991
Month 2 Payment	$	1,528
Next Months Principal Portion	$	464
Total Mortgage Payment for Month 2	$	1,992

Fig. 5. Loan repayment trick.

As you can see, because this method doesn't drastically increase your monthly mortgage payment, it is manageable. Your payment will increase incrementally over time, however, because the principal portion of the payment increases over time. This can help reduce the time it takes to pay down your debt and can save you thousands in interest in the long run with the bank. Specifically, in this example, you'd pay off your mortgage in 19 years as opposed to 30 and you would save more than $30,000 in interest payments. The bottom line is no matter how you do it, making principal payments toward your mortgage each month will help you in the long run. This trick helps you stick to a manageable prepayment schedule.

This method works particularly well as you continue to make a little more money over the life of the loan, especially if you have a sense of urgency to pay off the loan. It is always the goal to increase your income over time, and when you do so, this method can help you manage your payments in an efficient manner.

First-time homebuyer programs

Now that you know what's behind the bank financing, you may want to research online which first-time homebuyer programs are available. These programs can help you financially by managing your costs. Many federal, state, and local programs are designed to help first-time homebuyers with down payments, reduced interest rates, and other loan terms so that they may acquire the home they want. Research the Federal Housing Administration (FHA) resources. A few popular programs are as follows:

- FHA 203(b) Loan: This loan is made by a lending institution that is insured by the Department of Housing and Urban Development (HUD). The borrower must meet FHA credit qualifications and may be eligible for up to approximately 97%

financing (97% LTV). Most closing costs can be included in the loan, if the borrower qualifies. These loans also consider properties that are up to four units.

- HUD 203(k) Loan: This loan is designed to help buyers who need to make upgrades to the property they are buying. Like the 203(b) loan, this loan is made by a lending institution and is insured by HUD. It is a single, long-term fixed or adjustable rate loan that covers the acquisition and rehabilitation of the property. These loans save borrowers time and money compared with construction financing. They also protect the lender by having the loan insured before the borrower begins the property's renovation.

- Tax Credit: HUD has tax credit programs for first-time homebuyers that can allow them to monetize their tax credit upfront and put that credit toward the purchase of the property, if the loan is HUD insured. This credit can help alleviate the amount of out-of-pocket expenses required at closing.

Because of government policy changes over time, it is recommended that you research first-time homebuyer programs that aid you financially. You may be able to find local lenders that specialize in these programs and that can assist you in the process. You also can visit the HUD website to find out more at www.HUD.gov.

5. HOW TO NEGOTIATE THE PRICE YOU WANT

Now that you are ready to make an offer on a house, you should understand the market and the time at which a particular home has been listed. Meet with your realtor and get answers from them about what type of market it is, what the current home inventory is like, and what the weaknesses are in the market. The more you know about what is going on in the local housing market, the more informed you will be to make the best decisions.

Buyer's market

A buyer's market exists when more homes are being offered for sale than people are actively looking for homes to purchase. If you find yourself in this fortunate situation, you have leverage. You will not have to move as quickly to make an offer, compete with other buyers, or stress out about losing the house. You have the opportunity to put in a lower offer first and see where it goes. When you put in a low offer, always have in mind the maximum amount you will pay, and make sure that the amount is no higher than what you believe the value to be in that type of buyer's market (i.e., ensure that it is still a good deal relative to the asking price). Also, try not to get emotionally involved with a home. If you really like a home, don't let that feeling force you to make rash decisions. In a buyer's market, more homes like the one you like are out there, so stay calm and keep exploring all your options. Your realtor will help you through this, and don't be bashful about asking them questions.

In this type of market, you have the opportunity to walk away. With more homes on the market and limited buyers, there is a good chance that you will find another home that meets all of your requirements. Use this opportunity to your advantage and make a slightly lower offer. Pick a number that works for you and stick to it with minimal upward wiggle room. Tell the seller it is a standing offer and then go look at other homes. As long as you have no urgency to buy, don't pressure yourself in this market. Empower yourself with the feeling of control and be decisive. Chances are that you will like what you get when you keep your offer firm in this situation.

Understanding how long the home has been on the market and whether any previous offers have been made is important. The realtor you use might be able to find out how many offers have previously been made on the house you like and at what price. Getting information on previous offers may be hard; however, realtors talk and may have inside knowledge. If the listing has been active for more than six months, this increases your leverage even more. Remember, the house has been listed because the seller wants or needs to sell the property. After being on the market for six months without a sale, the seller may begin to feel weighed down and likely will get excited if they get any offer, even if it is lower than what they are asking.

If you follow this advice, you might get the sinking feeling that someone else could make a better offer, but don't worry about that. Have your real estate agent stay in contact with the selling agent so that you don't lose the opportunity if you really like the home. Chances are that if an offer comes in above yours, it wasn't that much higher. So, if that happens, stay engaged, know your max number, stick to it, and determine how you would like to proceed.

Also, a selling agent may try to pull a bluff. They may say that they got another offer or are expecting an offer from another party when in reality, this is not the case. It is a way of getting a little more out of you to increase the purchase price. You won't know whether or not it's true, but as mentioned, you need to know your max. Identify what you believe the max value of the home to be, so in the event you do encounter a little pressure, you can move up to a number that may be accepted by the seller while you still feel comfortable about the price.

Seller's market

If you are in a seller's market, more buyers are looking than homes are listed for sale. In this case, you may feel the urgency to buy and rush the process, so you really need to assess your situation. Do you feel the pressure to move? Do you need to buy, or can you continue to rent? Understand all of your options for your future living situation, and decide what makes you comfortable. If you are renting now, try to negotiate a month-to-month lease with your landlord. Be completely honest, especially if you have a good relationship with them. Let them know your plans. Chances are they will be willing to work with you and they will appreciate your honesty and communication. This offers you flexibility so that you don't have to feel rushed to buy or have to make rash decisions in a competitive market. With the flexibility of a short-term lease, you can look for a home and be well positioned to move out when you find that special home. If you need to buy a home and it happens to be a seller's market, you can take a few steps to prepare yourself and enable you to be more decisive in the search process:

1. Analyze your target market:

   - Analyze the comparable home sales

   - Know the average days on the market

   - Examine available inventory

   - Understand how close the actual sales prices are to the listing prices

2. Know your max number on each home based on your market analysis and your own personal value of the property.

3. Have your source of financing teed up and ready to go if you want to act.

No matter what the market conditions are when you are looking at homes, do the groundwork to position yourself well before you pull the trigger and make an offer. Follow these three steps to help you take control of your circumstances. This gives you the power to walk away and not be worried sick or act desperately when making decisions in this market.

The offer

When contemplating your offer number, always discuss this with your realtor. Your realtor will handle all of the paper-work involved with documenting an offer. Depending on the situation, you may need to show mortgage preapproval, make a 1% good faith deposit to be held in escrow, and acknowledge any disclosure paperwork provided by the seller. This is just preliminary stuff to get the ball rolling on the purchase process, and it is not binding. As long as you hire a competent realtor, he or she will guide you through the paperwork. Don't be afraid to lean on your realtor through this process and ask questions, it is the realtor's job to handle the technicalities of the purchase process to help you acquire your desired home.

Ask your realtor to review with you the list of homes that sold within the past year that are similar to the one you are considering. These are called "sales comparables," or in short, "comps." Be sure to ask for homes that were definitively sold within the past year—the more recent the sale, the better. This information will allow you to see what comparable homes in the immediate market actually sold for and will let you know whether the price you have in mind would be reasonable in the mind of the seller.

For example, consider the following hypothetical situation that can occur when making your offer:

Let's say that you examine the actual sales comps your agent provides on your target home, and on average, the past year's sales prices range from $395,000 to $410,000. If the home you like is listed at $420,000, then you know that the buyer is anchoring the price a little high and is likely prepared to negotiate downward. Negotiation is a bit like dancing and in order for both parties to feel like they've had a bit of fun, they both need to feel that they won. Believe it or not, if you swept in and paid $420,000 cash and cracked a bottle of champagne on the front lawn while high-fiving your broker, the seller likely would feel he lost the negotiation. Even though he got exactly what he wanted, he would think, "Oh no, I didn't ask enough." Similarly, if he accepted your $380,000 offer, and you drove by the house and the seller was laughing and rolling on the lawn, you might have a bit of buyer's remorse and think, "Oh no, I offered too much!" The most reasonably negotiated prices typically meet in the middle, and both parties feel psychologically more comfortable when they have both won a little and lost a little. It's going in the right direction when both parties are fighting for that agreeable number. And, this most often happens when the agreed-upon price is the fair price.

In this scenario, if you have done your homework, which undoubtedly you have, you would know that the maximum you want to spend on a home is $400,000. Consider offering $380,000 while knowing full well that the seller will counter at somewhere around $410,000, and you will have to adjust upward. Next, let us assume the seller counters at $415,000, and you move your price to $390,000. The seller calls your broker and says he would go to $408,000, and you would consider going to $395k. Then you might be at a standoff on the price, at which point the process could get a little tense. Remember, that is part of the fun. Keep them on their toes. They certainly will keep you on yours. It is a good idea that with every counter offer, you raise a concern with the house through your broker. Your broker might say to the selling agent, "My client is willing to go to $398,000 at this juncture. Would you please ask them about the driveway and front yard walkway? It is cracking in some parts and looks to be in need of repair. How long has that condition been that way? Have you had anyone give you a price on repairing that?" This will immediately justify your lower offer and begin to sow seeds of doubt in the mind of the seller.

Typically, finding that true market value will give you your target price. Most of the time, the seller is asking more than what that true market value actually would indicate. Make your offer below the estimated market value and control the situation to get the seller to that true market value price. The seller usually will be cognizant of the price at which comparable properties sold, and knows it is wise to come to a deal in that price range if they really want to sell the house.

This is exactly how you arrive at a deal. Remember, this is not a game of trying to short the other party. It is about getting to the right price that works for both parties. This is how true market value is determined. And it is why it is important to know the actual comp sales prices that are less than one year old. This information will get you to the right spot so that you can effectively execute the sale.

If you see weakness, or a desperate selling situation or distressed property, by all means go after it like a shark and take advantage of it. Maybe you can get a steal. But remember, sharks smell blood, so you probably will face a lot of competition acquiring that property. Do what you can to make a great deal, but remember that these so-called steals are hard to come by.

In some cases, when an agreement is reached, it "goes to binder". The binder is an agreement to protect the buyer's right to purchase the home until the inspections are complete.

Once the binder agreement is signed by both parties, the seller has an obligation to sell and not accept other offers, even if they are higher. The buyer has the option to buy, but they can receive a full refund of the deposit if the inspections, appraisal or mortgage contingencies are unsatisfactory. If these items go well, the closing can commence.

6. THE PROCESS OF CLOSING

You found your home, made an offer, and negotiated an agreed-upon purchase price. So now what? At this point, your agent will walk you through the process of closing. This is their job. But you can expect and should anticipate the following during the process of preclosing and closing.

Preclosing

- Have an experienced closing attorney lined up that can take care of and review all documentation. Make sure you put him or her in touch with your bank or lender as well so they can communicate throughout the process.

- Review your property description per town or city records and make sure your property lines are defined. Your attorney can help you with this. It is good to walk the property so you have an understanding of the property boundaries. Have your attorney check to see if a survey has been completed for the property and if there are any issues regarding boundary lines.

- Have a sample of your contract provided for your review and break down its parts in plain English with your attorney.

- Once the purchase price is agreed, you will need to negotiate and execute a contract or purchase agreement, which will bind the parties and set forth their respective responsibilities to complete the transaction. Typically, once this document is signed, a 10% good faith deposit is required and will be held in escrow by either the seller's counsel or the title company. This deposit may constitute a portion of your down payment. Once the deposit is placed in escrow, it is unlikely that such deposit will be returned, unless title issues, inspection issues, encumbrances on the property are identified or financing contingencies are not satisfied. Make sure your attorney reviews this contract and related documents so contingencies for financing, title, and encumbrances are incorporated to protect you and that the attorney clearly communicates such contingencies to you.

- Make sure all information on the home is sent to the lender that is underwriting your mortgage. The lender will need to have an appraisal conducted and possibly a property condition report as a review of their collateral. As mentioned earlier, you want this value coming in at your purchase price or higher. If the value comes in higher than your agreed purchase price, you can feel even better about your decision. If it comes in lower, the bank will stick to their agreed LTV terms, which means you will not receive as much money from the bank. Alternatively, if the appraisal comes in lower than the contracted purchase price, you can try to use this as an opportunity to negotiate a lower purchase price with the seller so it doesn't kill the deal. As a part of the bank's due diligence, they will conduct a title search to ensure that their collateral does not have any encumbrances. These are some of those big banker words, but it just means they are checking for anything that could put the bank at risk of not getting repaid. Examples of encumbrances include tax liens, mechanics liens, or even a prior mortgage.

- Bank final approval is typically a 30- to 45-day process; however, this process can take even longer depending on any outstanding items they need from you. If you can be organized and prompt in responding to the bank's requests, it will reduce the risk of slowing down the closing.

- You will need to call your insurance agent (this is recommended if you don't already have one) to obtain quotes from different insurance companies to insure your home. Your insurance agent will handle this process. This information is important to have before closing. You will need to have your home insured before closing.

- Make sure you have the additional 10%, or whatever percentage needed, to fulfill your down-payment requirement. This amount will be due at closing. Your attorney may collect the amount before closing and put it into escrow with the deposit.

Closing

- Once the bank has approved the mortgage, you can pick a date to close on the home.

- Make sure your homeowner's insurance is effective on the day of closing.

- Double check to ensure your attorney has all the documentation needed from you and the bank.

- Although the seller is likely an honest individual acting in good faith, you should arrange for a time either the evening before the closing or the morning of the closing to do a final walk-through of the property to ensure that everything is in the condition as required by the contract or purchase agreement.

- Depending on the language of the contract or purchase agreement, you may need to agree on utility adjustments with the seller, including, but not limited to oil, gas, water, and electric. It is also helpful to ask the seller to bring copies of all the latest utility invoices, along with proof that such invoices have been paid in full. The bank or the title company also may request that a small sum be held in escrow following closing to cover any unpaid utilities with an appropriate adjustment after the closing.

- When reviewing all of your information, *triple check* the wiring information if bank funds are being wired. Make sure routing numbers and account numbers are accurate and that the needed parties have those numbers displayed accurately on their forms. You don't need your funds ending up in Mogadishu.

- The attorneys will create a closing statement displaying all the debits and credits of the transaction. This statement highlights the details of funds in the transaction. Review this for accuracy and ask for clarification from your attorney on any items that are unclear.

- With e-mail, all closing matters can be organized and coordinated online, so you don't have to be at your own closing. Don't stress if the closing day needs to fall on a day that you are away. Just make sure that all of your signatures and paperwork are set with your attorney before closing. Always review and look things over to ensure that the i's have been dotted and t's have been crossed.

- Your attorney will receive funds from your bank or lender. These funds are the remainder of funds to make the home purchase. The funds should be in the attorney's escrow account before closing day.

- On closing day, the attorney will have everything coordinated and, ideally, everything should be in place to complete the closing. The funds will then be released to complete the transaction.

7. OWNERSHIP

Now that you have closed, you're a homeowner. Congratulations! You should be proud and celebrate. If you have been renting for a while, you may experience many new things that come with homeownership. But do not be worried, with just small adjustments, you may find yourself becoming a bit more handy. It's not like you are living in an apartment any longer. You own a house! You can do anything to it that you want to. So let your imagination run wild and have fun with the handy work and home improvements. If you are thinking, "absolutely not, I can't be bothered," then consider hiring someone to do all the little things around your home that need to be done each month. Just remember that hiring someone will be an added expense. After making your home purchase, you may want a short break from money outflows. So consider dabbling with little projects, and you will start getting better and better at improving the little things around your home. If you get into it, you actually could start building a good skill set, and who knows, you might actually fall in love with making these improvements on your home while also saving money in the process.

The Following is a list of the immediate things you need to know about your home as the owner:

Know the mechanical shutoffs

- Know where the furnace; boiler; and heating, ventilation, and air conditioning (HVAC) systems are located and identify the shutoff switches. When an HVAC contractor comes to service your system, ask that person to walk you through this step and show you any other important items you should know about your system.

- Know where your main water line is located, where it comes into the house, and how to shut it off.

- Know whether any water spigots or valves going to the exterior of your home need to be winterized. You do not want pipes to freeze or burst in the middle of a cold winter.

- Know where your electrical panel is located. Also know the electrical AMP power. In the event you blow a circuit, you will need to go to your electric panel and flip the circuit on, so ensure that all circuits are labeled correctly.

- If you have propane or natural gas, know where your supply line is located and know where the shutoff valve is.

- Know where the hot water heater is located and where the water and electric shutoffs are.

When you find a HVAC contractor, plumber, and electrician you like, these professionals can walk you through these points so that you know where everything is and can label them correctly. See the section "Find Tradespeople You Can Trust" in the upcoming pages.

Once you have these items located, label them clearly. These are the mechanicals of the home, and if anything should go wrong, you need to know where and how to shut them off. Some newer homes have mechanical rooms where most of these items can be located.

(a) Example of an oil-fueled furnace and gas HVAC unit

(b) Outdoor water spigot

(d) Gas manifolds and shutoffs in newer homes

(e) Example of electrical panel

(f) Hot water heater

Fig. 6. Mechanicals.

Know where the incoming utility lines are located

The utilities are what supplies energy to the mechanicals of your home. Utilities such as electric, water, and gas have to come in from the street to your home. You should know where these lines are located.

Electric

Most older homes will have overhead power lines that connect to the house from a street pole. You should identify which ones are the electrical lines. Don't confuse the lines with the telephone line, which many older homes will have. Generally, the electrical lines will be thicker and will be wrapped around or run with a steel cable. This is the line you don't want to mess with. You should have it marked so that you know it is the power line. Your electrician can assist you with this task.

If you have a newer home, you may have underground electric. If this is the case, you should know where these lines run from the street pole. These lines, by most codes, should be at least 36 inches below the surface. When buried, they are required to have a caution tape laying 12 inches below the surface directly over the line in case someone mistakenly is digging in the wrong spot. For that reason, it is important that you know where your underground electric lines are located in case you have any landscaping or excavating done at your home.

Water

Many homes have a water line that runs to the home from the street water main. This water line is usually a 1- to 2-inch-thick pipe that is buried about 48 inches below the surface. It is good to know where this line is for the same reason as the electric: you don't want to dig it up.

Some homes may have well water. In this case, one or more wells on the property may supply the home with water. You will want to know where the well(s) are located, where the lines are located that supply the home, and which meters, if any, are used to read the water levels. Some older wells may not have meters.

Gas

Newer homes are starting to use natural gas, and this is another utility line that will run from the street to your home. This line is generally buried 36 inches below the surface, per most codes. Like the electric, this should have caution tape 12 inches below the surface and directly over the line in case someone mistakenly is digging in the wrong spot.

If you don't have natural gas coming in from the street, you may have propane gas, and if so, this means you have a propane tank on your property. It may be above or below ground, but wherever it may be, it is important you know where the tanks are located and where the lines are located that go from the tanks to the house.

Most states have companies like Call Before You Dig (CBYD) that you call before you break ground so that your utility lines can be located and marked. These companies will contact the utility providers for your area and have them send out personnel to mark the utility lines with spray paint. You may have observed spray paint writing on roadways (on the actual asphalt) in your travels around construction sites, and this is exactly what those markings indicate. So any time you decide to have a major project completed at your house for which you know you will be breaking ground, make sure your contractor calls a CBYD service before starting the project. Safety always should be the number one priority.

Oil Tank and Lines

The oil tanks are set up similarly to propane tanks, and they will be located somewhere on your property. Depending on when and where your home was built, they could be above- or below ground. In most cases, the oil tank is in the basement of the home or directly on the outside of the house. The oil company will come regularly to fill the tank with oil. Based on consumption patterns, seasons, and weather, these oil companies usually keep your tanks filled before you would run out. Make sure this is the case when choosing your oil supplier. The tanks usually have a filling spout that allows for easy refilling access. From your tank, you generally have a copper line or pipe that will travel to your furnace. This line feeds your furnace oil. Know exactly where this line is, so that it doesn't mistakenly get cut or damaged if you decide to have a renovation or other work done on your home.

Additional lines to consider if you end up breaking ground in your backyard is the waste line that runs from your home to your septic tank or sewer as well as any irrigation lines if you have a sprinkler system servicing your lawns. Keep this in mind and locate these lines before you do any excavating.

Setting up your utility services

When you move into your home, you will have to identify your utility providers. Depending on where you live, what you need to do may vary. The electrical service is generally provided by a private utility company that covers the area in which you are located. You will need to research the providers and, if possible, see what price per kilowatt is being charged so you can select your most cost-effective option.

Water may be provided by your municipality or by a private water company that covers your area. Like the electric, you will need to research this service as well as gas (if you have natural gas).

If your home uses propane or oil, private companies generally will supply gas and oil and will service your furnace. These companies may fall under home fuel or HVAC companies. Some companies handle all aspects of home climate control, including fuel. So, research these home heating and HVAC businesses to provide fuel and to service your HVAC systems.

Find tradespeople you can trust

When you move into your home, you're going to need to find tradespeople you can trust to work on your home. These individuals should be able to address any work you may want to have completed or to fix any issues that may arise. You are the landlord now, so you need to get the right person in to repair the problem if something happens. If you don't already use specific tradespeople, consider a few good places to start:

- Ask any friends that live in the area if they have any good electricians, plumbers, or carpenters

with whom they have experience. Are they trustworthy, efficient, and affordable? Do they do
good work?

- Look online to see if you can find good reviews
  and check out company websites if they have
  them. *Note:* Sometimes some of the best tradespeople won't have websites, and this doesn't
  mean they are bad or inexperienced. It may be
  because they are a boutique and don't advertise.
  If you are referred to someone who doesn't have
  a website, it isn't necessarily a red flag, so don't
  dismiss this person as an option, instead ask for
  references and a portfolio of their work.

- Ask your realtor for recommendations. As mentioned earlier, the real estate industry is interconnected. Your realtor may be able to recommend
  quality tradespeople.

When you have identified the people you are comfortable with, you should request certificates of liability insurance
and contractor's licenses. Make sure these professionals are
insured and have worker's compensation insurance and that
they are qualified to do work on your home. Also, have your
contractors include you and your property as an "additional
insured" on their general liability policies. When you are an

additional insured, you are protected by the contractor's policy. In the event you are sued as a result of damage the contractor causes, their insurance company is required to cover the claim. Generally, when you request this from your contractor, they will call their insurance agent, and the insurance agent will send you an insurance certificate with you named as an additional insured. This will protect you in the unlikely event that something should go wrong.

Once you have the necessary documentation, create a list of trades with phone numbers to help you stay organized. As you become acclimated to your new home, you may continue to need minor work done. When this happens, you'll already know which contractors to use. You will get a feel for how they operate, how professional they are, the quality of their work, their honesty and client care. Build a rapport with them, especially if you are thinking about future upgrades to the home.

Become handy, if you aren't already

If you are moving from an apartment, you may need to develop handy skills. If that is so, don't let that stop you from learning. If you are trying to do minor things around your home like hanging pictures, fixing a door knob, changing an AC filter, or building a little shelf, just go for it. As mentioned earlier, you always can call a handy service for this type of work if you don't want to do it yourself (DIY), but if you want to save money, you should DIY. Seriously, this can be fun. During the week, create a small list of projects that you want to tackle and then allocate a couple hours on Saturday morning to get them done. If you are not sure how to do something, search for instructions on YouTube. You likely will find information about how to do exactly what you need to have done, and it will help you immensely. Also, observe the tools used, and if you don't have them, go to your local hardware store to get the tools you need. Build a work area in your basement or garage where you can keep your tools organized. Maybe you'll accumulate tools over time and then you can make yourself an awesome workbench. As you continue down this road, you'll discover a lot of possibilities.

Handy work brings out your creativity and your problem-solving skills. You already have creativity and problem-solving abilities, so don't dismiss yourself by saying or thinking you can't be handy. Don't be afraid to try some things around your house. You will find that if you start with some small stuff, you'll gain confidence and experience and soon will move to slightly bigger projects. If you enjoy it, you'll probably find yourself watching how-to videos online and networks like DIY and HGTV more often. Don't be afraid to try these things—you never know, you could be a natural.

8. HOW TO CREATE AND ADD VALUE TO YOUR HOME

When you buy a home, you are hoping it will be an appreciating asset for you and your family. You can change "hoping" into "making" it be an appreciating asset by doing the right things around the home. As you become handy, you won't have any issues with doing the right things. Consider a few ways to add value:

- **Interior maintenance:** Keep your home tidy and clean on a continuous basis. Clean up spills immediately, don't let things sit, and so on. Hire a cleaning professional if need be; it will be worth it to keep your home looking good on the interior. Also, with your new DIY abilities, stay on top of the interior paint, plaster, and molding. Keep your eyes open for any cracks and fix them as soon as they occur. This will keep your house in tip-top shape on the inside and will help you feel good as well.

- **Exterior maintenance:** If you do not know how to cut your lawn or landscape your yard, you can learn fast. It is not hard. If you can keep your exterior well landscaped, it makes your house look great. If needed, hire a landscaper to help. Keeping the property up goes a long way toward its resale value. The exterior provides the first impression when people view your home. Stay on top of the house façade, too, including a good paint job, clean windows, and well-conditioned roof. Try not to let things build up on the property, like the inside of your home, avoid clutter and stuff that can be an eyesore to neighbors, passersby, and, most important, you.

- **Interior upgrades:** The best upgrades you can make to your home for the most value added are bathroom, kitchen, and HVAC upgrades. If you have a home that needs a new master bath or kitchen, it is a good move to put money into upgrading them for resale purposes and, of course, for your enjoyment while you reside in your home. The HVAC system is important as well. When living in a home, people need comfortable temperature settings. A good system that gets to the desired temperature quickly and efficiently is a huge quality in a home.

Home upgrades

If you know you want to do a kitchen or a bath upgrade, consider the following to ensure that you plan for this work the right way:

- If you want to keep your plumbing in the existing spots, and won't be changing the layout, you may not need to do a drawing. This is considered a "cosmetic" upgrade, which means that you are not making any structural upgrades, adding new walls, or completely redesigning the home. If, however, you want to move things around, you will need to take measurements and create a plan to make sure it is dimensionally feasible. If you are doing a kitchen and want new cabinets, it is always good to take your room measurements and go to a kitchen cabinet retailer for a kitchen and cabinet design. Home Depot and Lowes both provide kitchen design services. You also can find independent kitchen professionals that can design and create your kitchen at competitive pricing.

• Look online at sites like Houzz and Pinterest to find styles and materials you like.

• Once you have an idea of what you want to do and the style you want to go with, have your carpenter walk through the room you want to upgrade. Show him or her photos of the style you like and ask what he or she would charge to demo the room and get it ready for the finish work. Also ask whether the carpenter has a good tile person and get that person to give you a quote as well. Have your plumber and electrician come in to give you a quote on fixture (toilet, sinks and lighting fixture) disconnects and hook-ups.

• When you get the quotes from your tradespeople, understand the quotes so that you know whether you're being quoted on labor, materials, or both. Make sure the quote is itemized and clear. If you feel the price is expensive, you have the right to get other quotes and compare them. When you do compare, make sure you are comparing apples to apples (i.e., they are quoting you on the same work scope). If you have any questions for them, don't be afraid to ask. You want to understand everything—the more you understand, the better.

- When you have a handle on the quotes to do the work and labor, start digging into the materials you will need to make the kitchen or bath have the features you desire. Price the cabinets, tiles, countertops, vanities, fixtures, and other finishes. It will be important to create a budget so you know what your costs will be to renovate and so that you can stick to these expenses through the renovation process. It is essential to keep to a budget because it is extremely easy to go overboard on materials and labor if you aren't conscious of your dollar amounts at all times. Consider the following basic examples of bathroom and kitchen renovation budgets for your reference:

Bathroom Renovation	
Budget Item	$
Dumpster	
Demolition	
Plumbing Fixture Disconnect	
Sheetrock & Cement Board	
Taping and Plaster	
Plumbing Fixtures (material)	
Tub	
Sink	
Vanity	
Shower head Faucet & Rough Connect	
Sink faucet and drain	
Floor Tile	
Wall Tile	
Medicine Cabinet (if applicable)	
Light Fixtures	
Exhaust Fan	
Paint	
Painter Labor	
Carpenter Labor	
Plumber Labor	
Electrician Labor	
Subtotal	
General Conditions (5%-8%)	
Total	

Kitchen Renovation	
Budget Item	$
Dumpster	
Demolition	
Plumbing Fixture Disconnect	
Sheetrock & Cement Board	
Insulation, Taping and Plaster	
Plumbing Fixtures (material)	
Sink	
Sink faucet and drain	
Garbage Disposal	
Appliances	
Stove and/or oven	
Hood and Exhaust Fan	
Refridgerator	
Dishwasher	
Microwave	
Flooring	
Wall Tile	
Cabinets	
Light Fixtures	
Countertops & Installation	
Paint	
Painter Labor	
Carpenter Labor	
Plumber Labor	
Electrician Labor	
Subtotal	
General Conditions (5%-8%)	
Total	

Fig. 7. Budget images.

Depending on where you order your plumbing and electrical fixtures, cabinets, countertops, and appliances, there is generally a decent lead time after you order them before delivery. You will want to coordinate these schedules with your tradespeople so that you know at what point to order these items. Have good communication with everyone working on your home so you can keep the project flowing at a good pace once you start it.

The general conditions line item accounts for overruns. The probability is high that something unexpected will come up during a renovation that adds a little more to the budget. A wall could be opened and rot might be discovered, or you could misjudge the tile material costs. These things happen, so it is good to allocate at least 5–8%, or higher to account for these unexpected costs.

Once you have your design, style, quotes, and budget compiled, and you feel comfortable to move forward with the renovation, check with your municipal building department because you may need to get permits before you commence work. The carpenter, plumber, and electricians sometimes pull the permits, but ask them how this will be handled.

Again, make sure your tradespeople are insured with liability insurance and worker's compensation and that they are licensed professionals capable of doing the work. Also, structure payments so that you pay based on work completed and to your satisfaction. Don't give any work deposits unless the contractor is purchasing materials for the project, and don't be bashful about this: have them show you material lists or invoices so you can watch every dollar and be sure to keep this organized.

If you are living in the home during the renovation, ask the carpenter to properly seal off the renovated area to limit the dust in your house. Specific types of painter's plastic and renovation sealing plastics act as walls to restrict dust and debris from entering other rooms.

When you have all this lined up, you are ready to renovate. Get excited about it; you are increasing your comfort level within your home and adding value with these type of upgrades.

If this is more than you want to handle or deal with, you can call a general contractor that can manage the process for you. They generally will charge 15–25% or more of the project cost. You also want to do your homework on these contractors to make sure they are insured, licensed, trustworthy, and reputable.

Home additions

If you want to expand the square footage of your home by adding a dormer, new wing of the house, or an additional floor, working with a general contractor is recommended. This is a more extensive process that will involve architectural drawings, engineering, and a lot more coordination than a simple bathroom or kitchen upgrade.

Your initial step should be to create a drawing of the work you want done. Even a chicken scratch drawing is a good starting point. Create a floor plan you like, and the exterior look and roof lines you want. Use resources such as architectural publications and online home sites to find design examples you like. These visuals are helpful for the architect. Then, once you have done that work, find an architect that specializes in home additions and make an appointment to see whether your design is structurally feasible. The architect probably will want to do a few walk-throughs of your home to get a feel for the property. Make sure the architect you choose knows your ballpark budget, so they know what you are willing to spend. From that point, they can work and see how close they can get to your design. Just like any other person who would be working on your home, it is recommended that you do your homework. Make sure you hire a certified architect. Always ask to review a photo portfolio of work. Also, see whether the person is a certified structural engineer or works closely with a reputable structural engineer that will be able to create and sign off on the structural specifications of the design.

If you find an architect you like and with whom you feel comfortable, they will present you a contract dollar amount for their services. Once it is agreed to and signed, you will be working with that architect for some time to create the design you like. Continue to find photos of what you like or would like to replicate and show your architect. This will help the design process move in the right direction. The design process may take a few weeks. Take the time to think about it and make sure it is what you really want. Once this work is done, the architect should work with the structural engineer to develop a plan to show all the structural supports of the new addition. This is also known as the framing plan. This plan labels all load-bearing beams, girders, types of beams, steel, and so on. This is important and ensures that the structure will meet the building codes and be safe to occupy.

Once the architectural plans are finalized, signed off, and labeled "for construction," you will need to build a budget similar to the ones displayed earlier. Generally, an addition has a larger scope and the budget will be more detailed. Your general contractor usually does this for you, and you can work with them on this, if you request. Get all preliminary documentation compiled to file for the permits needed for construction. You will have to go to your municipal building department and complete an application for the project so they can properly inspect the home at critical stages in the construction process. This will protect you by helping to ensure your home is being built to code and also will help for safety reasons. When you apply for your permits, depending on your town or city, you will complete paperwork for each department. You may need to fill out paperwork for the following departments: planning and zoning, health, conservation, building, and wetlands, if applicable. If you go to your town or city building department website, they may have a form displaying what paperwork you need to acquire for full department permit approval. With the application, you likely will need to submit your final "for construction" architectural plans, engineering plan, and survey. This is part of the package that the town or city needs to review. You can work with your general contractor to get all this paperwork filled out and submitted properly as well. Once everything is properly submitted and approved by the municipality, you will need to pay a permit fee to the municipality for the project. At that point, work can commence. It sounds like a lot, and that's because it is. That's why a lot of people are happy to pay a general contractor upward of 25% to handle the whole project properly.

Your contractor can take it from there, but stay in good communication with them, watch your budget, and emphasize to your contractor that if anything unexpected should arise during the process, he or she must inform you of the problem so that you can discuss the next steps. The last thing you want is for the contractor to run into an unexpected issue, just fix it the way they think is best, and then hit you with an unexpected $1,000-plus bill that isn't in your budget. So make sure you can be as open and honest with each other as possible. This will ensure that your project goes smoothly.

9. ENJOY IT, IT'S YOUR HOME

Your home is your life. You will sleep in it, relax in it, have family dinners in it, have family gatherings in it, host celebrations in it, raise your children in it, and maybe even run a business out of it. The list goes on. So many great things and memories will occur in your home and will be a huge part of your life. Remember this when you have to put the down payment on the house, or if you need to fix it up. Putting money or equity into your home is not a bad thing. The markets have been risky since 2008 and returns are no guarantee. If putting money into your home brings you more comfort in your life, creates nice curb appeal, adds functionality, and provides daily benefits and memories, shouldn't that be considered a significant return you get to experience day in and day out? You will be living in your home and experiencing a constant benefit from it. When it comes to living, you only get one bite at the apple. So, it is important that you do what you can to keep or make your home as comfortable for you and your family as desired. For this reason, never feel like you are wasting money on your home. Investing in your home is investing in your quality of life.

Enjoy your asset. You have accomplished a lot by making this home purchase. Be proud of it and make the most of your new home.

AUTHOR BIOGRAPHY

Ben Stefan is a real estate professional that graduated from the University of Connecticut with a major in Real Estate and Urban Economics. He started his career in commercial real estate banking and has over 10 years experience in commercial lending and asset management. Additionally, he has over 15 years experience in residential construction and home renovation. He is a licensed realtor and has completed multiple home renovations and sales. He is an avid golfer and outdoorsman. He resides with his wife Nicolette and their dog Faith in Connecticut.

A special thank you

This is a special thank you to the following people that helped me along the way while writing this book. Your help was integral and is much appreciated.

Bill and Janet Stefan	Martin Rogers
Robert and Maggi Rogers	Lori Stefan
Nicolette Corrao	Chris Stefan
Pete Gunthel	Helen Stefan
Zach Lyon	David Stefan
Steve and Jenn Hubina	Tim Romano
Bob Proctor	Sally Bohling
Al Mazur	Jim DeVito
Marcy Ramsey	John Jones
Bob Rogers	Nick Renzulli
Lucy Montgomery	Matt DiPasquale
Jackie Rogers	Mark Brockwell

NOTES:

NOTES:

NOTES:

NOTES:

NOTES: